The PROPHETS SPEAK

FROM THE HOLY SCRIPTURES

The PROPHETS SPEAK

FROM THE HOLY SCRIPTURES

Compiled by
Leena Arthur

Media**Serve**

THE PROPHETS SPEAK
First published in English 1999
This edition published 2005

ISBN 0 9534793 3 1

Printed in India for MediaServe
www.mediaserve.org

Acknowledgments

Scripture quotations are taken from the
Holy Bible, New International Version® NIV®
(NIV), copyright © 1973, 1978, 1984 by
International Bible Society. Used by permission.
All rights reserved;
King James Version (KJV);
New American Standard Bible® (NASB),
copyright © 1960, 1962, 1963, 1968, 1971,
1972, 1973, 1975, 1977, 1995 by The Lockman
Foundation. Used by permission;
New Revised Standard Version (NRSV),
copyright © 1989 by Division of Christian Education
of the National Council of the Churches of Christ
in the United States of America. Used by
permission. All rights reserved;
Revised Standard Version of the Bible (RSV),
copyright © 1952, 1971 by Division of
Christian Education of the National Council of
the Churches of Christ in the United States of
America. Used by permission. All rights reserved;
New King James Version (NKJV),
copyright © 1982 by Thomas Nelson, Inc.
Used by permission. All rights reserved

Jacket illustration, Helena Backmark
Graphic design, Jessica Nyström

TO THE READER

Dear Friend,

This book is dedicated to all Jewish people throughout the world.

More than 2,500 years ago, the prophets Jeremiah, Isaiah and Ezekiel, and others like them, spoke not only to the Jewish people of their time, but to us too. They saw into our days and foretold many events that are taking place right here and now:

- *The birth* OF THE NATION OF ISRAEL

- *The exodus* OF JEWISH PEOPLE FROM ALL CORNERS OF THE EARTH

- *The transformation* OF THE LAND OF ISRAEL FROM A BARREN LAND INTO A GARDEN OF EDEN— AND MORE

Every word from God will be fulfilled—even if it takes centuries!

First you can read a selection of God's promises to the Jewish people, concerning their future and their land. Many promises have already been fulfilled, while others are coming to pass in amazing ways in front of our eyes. Through the prophet Isaiah, God says, "So is my word that goes out from my mouth: It will not return to me empty, but will accomplish what I desire and achieve the purpose for which I sent it" (Isaiah 55:11 NIV).

As you read this book, remember that God has good plans for his people and he will accomplish what he has said. Read these pages prayerfully and see how you fit into the plans of the God of Israel.

May the God of Abraham, Isaac and Jacob bless you!

The Publisher

CONTENTS

1

GOD'S PROMISES
TO THE JEWS

PROMISE OF A LAND

GOD'S PROMISE TO ABRAHAM

Now the LORD said to Abram,
"Go forth from your country,
And from your relatives
And from your father's house,
To the land which I will show you;
And I will make you a great nation,
And I will bless you,
And make your name great;
And so you shall be a blessing;
And I will bless those who bless you,
And the one who curses you I will curse.
And in you all the families of the earth will be blessed."

Genesis 12:1-3 NASB

"And I will establish my covenant between me and you and your descendants after you in their generations, for an everlasting covenant, to be God to you and your descendants after you. Also I give to you and your descendants after you the land in which you are a stranger, all the land of Canaan, as an everlasting possession; and I will be their God."

Genesis 17:7,8 NKJV

GOD'S PROMISE TO ISAAC

"Sarah your wife will bear you a son, and you shall call his name Isaac; and I will establish my covenant with him for an everlasting covenant for his descendants after him."

Genesis 17:19 NASB

"Dwell in this land, and I will be with you and bless you; for to you and your descendants I give all these lands, and I will perform the oath which I swore to Abraham your father."

Genesis 26:3 NKJV

GOD'S PROMISE TO JACOB

Then Jacob said to Joseph:
"God Almighty appeared to me at Luz in the land of Canaan and blessed me, and said to me, 'Behold, I will make you fruitful and multiply you, and I will make of you a multitude of people, and give this land to your descendants after you as an everlasting possession.'"

Genesis 48:3,4 NKJV

GOD'S PROMISE TO MOSES

The LORD spoke to Moses that very same day, saying, "Go up to this mountain of the Abarim, Mount Nebo, which is in the land of Moab opposite Jericho, and look at the land of Canaan, which I am giving to the sons of Israel for a possession."

Deuteronomy 32:48,49 NASB

PROMISE OF
AN ETERNAL COVENANT
WITH ISRAEL

"The people whom I formed for myself will declare my praise."

Isaiah 43:21 NASB

"And in you all the families of the earth will be blessed."

Genesis 12:3 NASB

"The LORD will establish you as a holy people to himself, as he swore to you, if you keep the commandments of the LORD your God and walk in his ways. So all the peoples of the earth will see that you are called by the name of the LORD, and they will be afraid of you."

Deuteronomy 28:9,10 NASB

The LORD appeared to him from afar, saying,
"I have loved you with an everlasting love;
Therefore I have drawn you with lovingkindness.
Again I will build you and you will be rebuilt,
O virgin of Israel!"

Jeremiah 31:3,4 NASB

Thus says the LORD,
Who gives the sun for light by day
And the fixed order of the moon
and the stars for light by night,
Who stirs up the sea so that its waves roar;
The LORD of hosts is his name:
"If this fixed order departs
From before me," declares the LORD,
"Then the offspring of Israel also will cease
From being a nation before me forever."

Jeremiah 31:35,36 NASB

"Remember these things, O Jacob,
And Israel, for you are my servant;
I have formed you, you are my servant,
O Israel, you will not be forgotten by me."

Isaiah 44:21 NASB

PROMISE TO RESTORE THE NATION

Comfort, comfort my people,
says your God.
Speak tenderly to Jerusalem,

and proclaim to her
that her hard service has been completed,
that her sin has been paid for,
that she has received from the LORD's hand
double for all her sins.

Isaiah 40:1,2 NIV

"For I know the plans I have for you," declares the Lord, "plans to prosper you and not to harm you, plans to give you hope and a future."

Jeremiah 29:11 NIV

GOD'S PEOPLE, THE JEWS, WILL BE RESTORED

On that day the Lord will extend his hand yet a second time to recover the remnant that is left of his people.... He will raise a signal for the nations, and will assemble the outcasts of Israel, and gather the dispersed of Judah from the four corners of the earth.

Isaiah 11:11,12 NRSV

"For I will take you from the nations, gather you from all the lands and bring you into your own land. Then I will sprinkle clean water on you, and you will be clean; I will cleanse you from all your filthiness and from all your idols. Moreover, I will give you a new heart and put a new spirit within you; and I will remove the heart of stone from your flesh and give you a heart of flesh. I will put

my Spirit within you and cause you to walk in
my statutes, and you will be careful to observe my
ordinances. You will live in the land that I gave to
your forefathers; so you will be my people, and I
will be your God."

Ezekiel 36:24-28 NASB

"At that time I will gather you;
at that time I will bring you home.
I will give you honor and praise
among all the peoples of the earth
when I restore your fortunes
before your very eyes," says the LORD.

Zephaniah 3:20 NIV

BIRTH OF THE STATE OF ISRAEL

"Who has heard such a thing?
Who has seen such things?
Can a land be born in one day?
Can a nation be brought forth all at once?
As soon as Zion travailed,
she also brought forth her sons."

Isaiah 66:8 NASB

JERUSALEM WILL BE ESTABLISHED

On your walls, O Jerusalem,
I have appointed watchmen;
All day and all night
they will never keep silent.

You who remind the LORD,
take no rest for yourselves;
And give him no rest until he establishes
And makes Jerusalem a praise in the earth.

Isaiah 62:6,7 NASB

Pray for the peace of Jerusalem:
"May they prosper who love you."
For the sake of the house of the LORD our God,
I will seek your good.

Psalm 122:6,9 NASB

Jerusalem will be trampled under foot by the
Gentiles until the times of the Gentiles are fulfilled.

Luke 21:24 NASB

INHERITANCE RESTORED

"In those days the house of Judah will walk with
the house of Israel, and they will come together
from the land of the north to the land that I gave
your fathers as an inheritance."

Jeremiah 3:18 NASB

PROMISE TO GATHER ISRAEL

Hear the word of the LORD, O nations,
And declare in the coastlands afar off,
And say, "He who scattered Israel will gather him
And keep him as a shepherd keeps his flock."
For the LORD has ransomed Jacob
And redeemed him from the hand of him
who was stronger than he.
"They will come and shout for joy
on the height of Zion,
And they will be radiant
over the bounty of the LORD —
Over the grain and the new wine and the oil,
And over the young of the flock and the herd;
And their life will be like a watered garden,
And they will never languish again."

Jeremiah 31:10-12 NASB

"Then I myself will gather the remnant of my
flock out of all the countries where I have driven
them and bring them back to their pasture, and
they will be fruitful and multiply."

Jeremiah 23:3 NASB

GOD CANNOT FORGET
HIS PEOPLE

"Behold, these will come from afar;
And lo, these will come from the north
and from the west,
And these from the land of Sinim."
Shout for joy, O heavens! And rejoice, O earth!
Break forth into joyful shouting, O mountains!
For the LORD has comforted his people
And will have compassion on his afflicted.
But Zion said, "The LORD has forsaken me,
And the Lord has forgotten me."
"Can a woman forget her nursing child
And have no compassion on the son of her womb?
Even these may forget, but I will not forget you.
Behold, I have inscribed you
on the palms of my hands;
Your walls are continually before me."

Isaiah 49:12-16 NASB

GENTILES HELP TO BRING JEWS
TO ISRAEL

Thus says the Lord GOD,
"Behold, I will lift up my hand to the nations
And set up my standard to the peoples;
And they will bring your sons in their bosom,
And your daughters will be carried on their
shoulders."

Isaiah 49:22 NASB

The LORD will have compassion on Jacob;
once again he will choose Israel
and will settle them in their own land.
Aliens will join them
and unite with the house of Jacob.
Nations will take them
and bring them to their own place.

Isaiah 14:1,2 NIV

"Foreigners will build up your walls,
And their kings will minister to you;
For in my wrath I struck you,
And in my favor I have had compassion on you."

Isaiah 60:10 NASB

"Kings will be your guardians,
And their princesses your nurses.
They will bow down to you
with their faces to the earth
And lick the dust of your feet;
And you will know that I am the LORD;
Those who hopefully wait for me
will not be put to shame."

Isaiah 49:23 NASB

"Do not fear, for I am with you;
I will bring your offspring from the east,
And gather you from the west.
I will say to the north, 'Give them up!'
And to the south, 'Do not hold them back.'

Bring my sons from afar
And my daughters from the ends of the earth,
Everyone who is called by my name,
And whom I have created for my glory,
Whom I have formed, even whom I have made."
Bring out the people who are blind,
even though they have eyes,
And the deaf, even though they have ears.

Isaiah 43:5-8 NASB

Then he said to me:
"Son of man, these bones are the whole house of Israel. They say, 'Our bones are dried up and our hope is gone; we are cut off.' Therefore prophesy and say to them: 'This is what the Sovereign LORD says: O my people, I am going to open your graves and bring you up from them; I will bring you back to the land of Israel. Then you, my people, will know that I am the LORD, when I open your graves and bring you up from them. I will put my Spirit in you and you will live, and I will settle you in your own land. Then you will know that I the LORD have spoken, and I have done it, declares the LORD.'"

Ezekiel 37:11-14 NIV

TO ZION WITH JOY

So the ransomed of the LORD shall return,
And come to Zion with singing,
With everlasting joy on their heads.

They shall obtain joy and gladness;
Sorrow and sighing shall flee away.

Isaiah 51:11 NKJV

Oh give thanks to the LORD, for he is good,
For his lovingkindness is everlasting.
Let the redeemed of the LORD say so,
Whom he has redeemed from the hand of the
adversary
And gathered from the lands,
From the east and from the west,
From the north and from the south.

Psalm 107:1-3 NASB

SHIPS AND AIRPLANES BRING IMMIGRANTS

"Lift up your eyes and look about you:
All assemble and come to you;
your sons come from afar,
and your daughters are carried on the arm.
Then you will look and be radiant,
your heart will throb and swell with joy;
the wealth on the seas will be brought to you,
to you the riches of the nations will come."

"Who are these that fly along like clouds,
like doves to their nests?
Surely the islands look to me;
in the lead are the ships of Tarshish,
bringing your sons from afar,

with their silver and gold,
to the honor of the LORD your God,
the Holy One of Israel,
for he has endowed you with splendor."

Isaiah 60:4,5,8,9 NIV

PREPARE THE WAY

"Set up for yourself roadmarks,
Place for yourself guideposts;
Direct your mind to the highway,
The way by which you went.
Return, O virgin of Israel,
Return to these your cities."

Jeremiah 31:21 NASB

Pass through, pass through the gates!
Prepare the way for the people.
Build up, build up the highway!
Remove the stones.
Raise a banner for the nations.
The LORD has made proclamation
to the ends of the earth:
"Say to the Daughter of Zion,
'See, your Savior comes!
See, his reward is with him,
and his recompense accompanies him.'"

Isaiah 62:10,11 NIV

A MIRACLE: RUSSIAN JEWS
RETURN TO ISRAEL

"Therefore, behold, the days are coming, says the LORD, when it shall no longer be said, 'As the LORD lives who brought up the people of Israel out of the land of Egypt,' but 'As the LORD lives who brought up the people of Israel out of the north country and out of all the countries where he had driven them.' For I will bring them back to their own land which I gave to their fathers. Behold, I am sending for many fishers, says the LORD, and they shall catch them; and afterwards I will send for many hunters, and they shall hunt them from every mountain and every hill, and out of the clefts of the rocks."

Jeremiah 16:14-16 RSV

"Up, up! Flee from the land of the north," says the LORD; "for I have spread you abroad like the four winds of heaven," says the LORD. "Up, Zion! Escape, you who dwell with the daughter of Babylon." For thus says the LORD of hosts: "He sent me after glory, to the nations which plunder you; for he who touches you touches the apple of his eye."

Zechariah 2:6-8 NKJV

"Therefore behold, the days are coming," declares the LORD, "when they will no longer say, 'As the LORD lives, who brought up the sons of Israel from the land of Egypt,' but, 'As the LORD lives, who brought up and led back the descendants of the household of Israel from the north land and from all the countries where I had driven them.' Then they will live on their own soil."

Jeremiah 23:7,8 NASB

PROMISE OF A FUTURE

Thus says the LORD,
"Restrain your voice from weeping
And your eyes from tears;
For your work will be rewarded," declares the LORD,
"And they will return from the land of the enemy.
There is hope for your future," declares the LORD,
"And your children will return to their own territory."

Jeremiah 31:16,17 NASB

A LAND OF BLESSING

"At that time I will bring you back,
Even at the time I gather you;
For I will give you fame and praise
Among all the peoples of the earth,
When I return your captives before your eyes,"
Says the LORD.

Zephaniah 3:20 NKJV

"On that day I will raise up
The tabernacle of David, which has fallen down,
And repair its damages;
I will raise up its ruins,
And rebuild it as in the days of old;
That they may possess the remnant of Edom,
And all the Gentiles who are called by my name,"
Says the LORD who does this thing.
    "Behold, the days are coming,"
says the LORD,
"When the plowman shall overtake the reaper,
And the treader of grapes him who sows seed;
The mountains shall drip with sweet wine,
And all the hills shall flow with it.
I will bring back the captives of my people Israel;
They shall build the waste cities and inhabit them;
They shall plant vineyards
and drink wine from them;
They shall also make gardens
and eat fruit from them.
I will plant them in their land,

And no longer shall they be pulled up
From the land I have given them,"
Says the LORD your God.

Amos 9:11-15 NKJV

THE DESERT WILL BE GLAD

"But you, O mountains of Israel, you will put forth your branches and bear your fruit for my people Israel; for they will soon come.

"For, behold, I am for you, and I will turn to you, and you will be cultivated and sown.

"I will multiply men on you, all the house of Israel, all of it; and the cities will be inhabited and the waste places will be rebuilt."

Ezekiel 36:8-10 NASB

The desert and the parched land will be glad;
the wilderness will rejoice and blossom.
Like the crocus, it will burst into bloom;
it will rejoice greatly and shout for joy.
The glory of Lebanon will be given to it,
the splendor of Carmel and Sharon;
they will see the glory of the LORD,
the splendor of our God.
Strengthen the feeble hands,
steady the knees that give way;
say to those with fearful hearts,
"Be strong, do not fear;
your God will come,
he will come with vengeance;

with divine retribution
he will come to save you."

Isaiah 35:1-4 <small>NIV</small>

"I will open rivers on the bare heights,
and fountains in the midst of the valleys;
I will make the wilderness a pool of water,
· and the dry land springs of water.
I will put in the wilderness the cedar,
the acacia, the myrtle, and the olive;
I will set in the desert the cypress,
the plane and the pine together;
that men may see and know,
may consider and understand together,
that the hand of the LORD has done this,
the Holy One of Israel has created it."

Isaiah 41:18-20 <small>RSV</small>

ANCIENT CITIES WILL BE REBUILT

The Spirit of the Lord GOD is upon me,
Because the LORD has anointed me
To bring good news to the afflicted;
He has sent me to bind up the brokenhearted,
To proclaim liberty to captives
And freedom to prisoners;
To proclaim the favorable year of the LORD
And the day of vengeance of our God;
To comfort all who mourn,

To grant those who mourn in Zion,
Giving them a garland instead of ashes,
The oil of gladness instead of mourning,
The mantle of praise instead of a spirit of fainting.
So they will be called oaks of righteousness,
The planting of the LORD, that he may be glorified.
Then they will rebuild the ancient ruins,
They will raise up the former devastations;
And they will repair the ruined cities,
The desolations of many generations.

Isaiah 61:1-4 NASB

"Thus says the Lord GOD: On the day that I cleanse you from all your iniquities, I will cause the cities to be inhabited, and the waste places shall be rebuilt. And the land that was desolate shall be tilled, instead of being the desolation that it was in the sight of all who passed by. And they will say, 'This land that was desolate has become like the garden of Eden; and the waste and desolate and ruined cities are now inhabited and fortified.'"

Ezekiel 36:33-35 RSV

"They shall dwell in the land where your fathers dwelt that I gave to my servant Jacob; they and their children and their children's children shall dwell there for ever; and David my servant shall be their prince for ever."

Ezekiel 37:25 RSV

COVENANT RENEWED

"The time is coming," declares the LORD,
"when I will make a new covenant
with the house of Israel
and with the house of Judah.
It will not be like the covenant
I made with their forefathers
when I took them by the hand
to lead them out of Egypt,
because they broke my covenant,
though I was a husband to them,"
declares the LORD.
    "This is the covenant I will make
with the house of Israel
after that time," declares the LORD.
"I will put my law in their minds
and write it on their hearts.
I will be their God,
and they will be my people.
No longer will a man teach his neighbor,
or a man his brother, saying, 'Know the LORD,'
because they will all know me,
from the least of them to the greatest,"
declares the LORD.
"For I will forgive their wickedness
and will remember their sins no more."

Jeremiah 31:31-34 NIV

THE NEW TESTAMENT
CONFIRMS
GOD'S PROMISES
TO THE JEWS

"You are sons of the prophets, and of the covenant which God made with our fathers, saying to Abraham, 'And in your seed all the families of the earth shall be blessed.'"

Acts 3:25 NKJV

They are Israelites, and to them belong the sonship, the glory, the covenants, the giving of the law, the worship, and the promises.

Romans 9:4 RSV

Has God rejected his people? By no means! ... As regards election they are beloved for the sake of their forefathers. For the gifts and the call of God are irrevocable.

Romans 11:1,28,29 RSV

What advantage has the Jew? Or what is the value of circumcision? Much in every way. To begin with, the Jews are entrusted with the oracles of God. What if some were unfaithful? Does their

faithlessness nullify the faithfulness of God? By no means!

Romans 3:1-4 RSV

He [Messiah] came and preached peace to you who were far off [Gentiles] and peace to those who were near [Jews]; for through him we both have access in one Spirit to the Father.

Ephesians 2:17,18 RSV

2

THE PROPHET ISAIAH SPEAKS OF MESSIAH

THE COMING
OF MESSIAH

HIS BIRTH

"The Lord himself will give you a sign: Behold, a virgin will be with child and bear a son, and she will call his name Immanuel."

Isaiah 7:14 NASB

HIS FAMILY

There shall come forth a shoot from the stump of Jesse, and a branch shall grow out of his roots.

Isaiah 11:1 RSV

HIS ANOINTING

The Spirit of the LORD shall rest upon him, the spirit of wisdom and understanding, the spirit of counsel and might, the spirit of knowledge and the fear of the LORD.

Isaiah 11:2 RSV

THE MISSION
OF MESSIAH

TO BE LIGHT IN DARKNESS

The people who walked in darkness have seen a
great light; those who lived in a land of deep darkness—on them light has shined.

Isaiah 9:2 NRSV

TO JUDGE RIGHTEOUSLY

He shall not judge by what his eyes see, or decide
by what his ears hear; but with righteousness he
shall judge the poor.

Isaiah 11:3,4 RSV

TO ESTABLISH LAW

He will not fail or be discouraged till he has established justice in the earth; and the coastlands wait
for his law.

Isaiah 42:4 RSV

TO LIBERATE

I am the LORD… I have given you as a covenant
to the people…to bring out the prisoners from the

dungeon, from the prison those who sit in darkness.

Isaiah 42:6,7 NRSV

TO CARRY OUR SORROWS

Surely he took up our infirmities and carried our sorrows, yet we considered him stricken by God, smitten by him, and afflicted.

Isaiah 53:4 NIV

TO TAKE AWAY OUR SIN

All we like sheep have gone astray; we have all turned to our own way, and the LORD has laid on him the iniquity of us all.

Isaiah 53:6 NRSV

TO INTERCEDE

Therefore I will divide him a portion with the great, and he shall divide the spoil with the strong; because he poured out his soul to death, and was numbered with the transgressors; yet he bore the sin of many, and made intercession for the transgressors.

Isaiah 53:12 RSV

TO BE OUR SAVIOR

But he was wounded for our transgressions, he was bruised for our iniquities; upon him was the chastisement that made us whole, and with his stripes we are healed.

Isaiah 53:5 RSV

THE NAMES
OF MESSIAH

IMMANUEL

A young woman shall conceive and bear a son, and
shall call his name Immanuel.

Isaiah 7:14 RSV

WONDERFUL COUNSELOR
MIGHTY GOD
EVERLASTING FATHER
PRINCE OF PEACE

For to us a child is born, to us a son is given; and
the government will be upon his shoulder, and
his name will be called "Wonderful Counselor,
Mighty God, Everlasting Father, Prince of Peace."

Isaiah 9:6 RSV

RIGHTEOUS KING

Behold, a king will reign in righteousness, and
princes will rule with justice.

Isaiah 32:1 NKJV

SERVANT

"Here is my servant, whom I uphold, my chosen one in whom I delight; I will put my Spirit on him and he will bring justice to the nations."

Isaiah 42:1 NIV
(Also Isaiah 53:11)

ARM OF THE LORD

Who has believed our message? And to whom has the arm of the LORD been revealed?

Isaiah 53:1 NASB

THE ANOINTED ONE

The Spirit of the Lord GOD is upon me,
Because the LORD has anointed me
To bring good news to the afflicted;
He has sent me to bind up the brokenhearted,
To proclaim liberty to captives
And freedom to prisoners.

Isaiah 61:1 NASB

MIGHTY VINDICATOR

Who is this that comes from Edom, in crimsoned garments from Bozrah, he that is glorious in his apparel, marching in the greatness of his strength? "It is I, announcing vindication, mighty to save."

Isaiah 63:1 RSV

THE CHARACTERISTICS OF MESSIAH

WISDOM

The spirit of the LORD shall rest upon him, the spirit of wisdom and understanding, the spirit of counsel and might, the spirit of knowledge and of the fear of the LORD.

Isaiah 11:2 KJV

SPIRITUAL DISCERNMENT

His delight shall be in the fear of the LORD. He shall not judge by what his eyes see, or decide by what his ears hear.

Isaiah 11:3 RSV

JUSTICE

With righteousness he shall judge the poor, and decide with equity for the meek of the earth; and he shall smite the earth with the rod of his mouth, and with the breath of his lips he shall slay the wicked.

Isaiah 11:4 RSV

RIGHTEOUSNESS

Righteousness shall be the belt around his waist,
and faithfulness the belt around his loins.

Isaiah 11:5 NRSV

MILD MANNERED

He will not cry out or raise his voice,
Nor make his voice heard in the street.

Isaiah 42:2 NASB

GENTLENESS

A bruised reed he will not break, and a dimly
burning wick he will not quench; he will faithfully
bring forth justice.

Isaiah 42:3 RSV

PERSEVERANCE

He will not fail nor be discouraged,
Till he has established justice in the earth;
And the coastlands shall wait for his law.

Isaiah 42:4 NKJV

COMPASSION

Surely he has borne our infirmities and carried our
diseases; yet we accounted him stricken, struck
down by God, and afflicted.

Isaiah 53:4 NRSV

MEEKNESS

He was oppressed, and he was afflicted, yet he did not open his mouth; like a lamb that is led to the slaughter, and like a sheep that before its shearers is silent, so he did not open his mouth.

Isaiah 53:7 NRSV

SINLESSNESS

He was assigned a grave with the wicked, and with the rich in his death, though he had done no violence, nor was any deceit in his mouth.

Isaiah 53:9 NIV

SUBSTITUTIONARY SUFFERING

It was the will of the LORD to bruise him; he has put him to grief; when he makes himself an offering for sin, he shall see his offspring, he shall prolong his days; the will of the LORD shall prosper in his hand.

Isaiah 53:10 RSV

SAVING POWER

He shall see the fruit of the travail of his soul and be satisfied; by his knowledge shall the righteous one, my servant, make many to be accounted righteous; and he shall bear their iniquities.

Isaiah 53:11 RSV

GREATNESS

Therefore I will divide him a portion with the
great, and he shall divide the spoil with the strong;
because he poured out his soul to death, and was
numbered with the transgressors; yet he bore the
sin of many, and made intercession for the transgressors.

Isaiah 53:12 RSV

3

PROPHECIES OF MESSIAH FULFILLED IN YESHUA

PROPHECIES OF MESSIAH FULFILLED IN YESHUA

SEED OF A WOMAN

Prophecy

"I will put enmity between you and the woman, and between your seed and her Seed; he shall bruise your head, and you shall bruise his heel."

Genesis 3:15 NKJV

Fulfillment

But when the fullness of the time had come, God sent forth his Son, born of a woman, born under the law.

Galatians 4:4 NKJV
(Also Luke 2:7; Revelation 12:5)

PROMISED SEED OF ABRAHAM

Prophecy

Abraham will surely become a great and powerful nation, and all nations on earth will be blessed through him.

Genesis 18:18 NIV
(Also Genesis 12:3)

Fulfillment

"You are the sons of the prophets and of the covenant which God gave to your fathers, saying to Abraham, 'And in your posterity shall all the families of the earth be blessed.'"

Acts 3:25 RSV
(Also Matthew 1:1; Luke 3:34)

PROMISED SEED OF ISAAC

Prophecy

God said, "No, but Sarah your wife will bear you a son, and you shall call his name Isaac; and I will establish my covenant with him for an everlasting covenant for his descendants after him."

Genesis 17:19 NASB

Fulfillment

The record of the genealogy of Jesus [Yeshua] the Messiah, the son of David, the son of Abraham: Abraham was the father of Isaac, Isaac the father of Jacob, and Jacob the father of Judah and his brothers.

Matthew 1:1,2 NASB

PROMISED SEED OF JACOB

Prophecy

"I see him, but not now;
I behold him, but not near;
A Star shall come out of Jacob;

A Scepter shall rise out of Israel,
And batter the brow of Moab,
And destroy all the sons of tumult."

Numbers 24:17 NKJV

Fulfillment

The son of Jacob, the son of Isaac, the son of Abraham, the son of Terah, the son of Nahor.

Luke 3:34 NKJV

HE WILL DESCEND FROM THE TRIBE OF JUDAH

Prophecy

The scepter shall not depart from Judah, nor the ruler's staff from between his feet, until tribute comes to him; and the obedience of the peoples is his.

Genesis 49:10 NRSV

Fulfillment

The son of Amminadab, the son of Admin, the son of Ram, the son of Hezron, the son of Perez, the son of Judah....

Luke 3:33 NASB
(Also Matthew 1:2,3)

THE HEIR TO THE THRONE
OF DAVID

Prophecy

Of the increase of his government and of peace
there will be no end, upon the throne of David,
and over his kingdom, to establish it, and to
uphold it with justice and with righteousness from
this time forth and for evermore. The zeal of the
LORD of hosts will do this.

Isaiah 9:7 RSV
(Also Isaiah 11:1-5; 2 Samuel 7:13)

Fulfillment

Jesus the Messiah, the son of David, the son of
Abraham.

Matthew 1:1 NASB
(Also Luke 1:32,33)

PLACE OF BIRTH

Prophecy

"But you, Bethlehem Ephrathah, though you are
small among the clans of Judah, out of you will
come for me one who will be ruler over Israel,
whose origins are from of old, from ancient
times."

Micah 5:2 NIV

Fulfillment

After Jesus was born in Bethlehem of Judea in the

days of Herod the king, behold, wise men from the East came to Jerusalem, saying, "Where is he who has been born King of the Jews? For we have seen his star in the East and have come to worship him."

Matthew 2:1,2 NKJV
(Also Luke 2:4,5,7)

TIME OF BIRTH

Prophecy
"Know therefore and understand,
That from the going forth of the command
To restore and build Jerusalem
Until Messiah the Prince,
There shall be seven weeks
and sixty-two weeks;
The street shall be built again,
and the wall,
Even in troublesome times."

Daniel 9:25 NKJV

Fulfillment
In those days a decree went out from Emperor Augustus that all the world should be registered. This was the first registration and was taken while Quirinius was governor of Syria.

Luke 2:1,2 NRSV
(Also Luke 2:3-7)

BORN OF A VIRGIN

Prophecy

The Lord himself will give you a sign: The virgin will be with child and will give birth to a son, and will call him Immanuel.

Isaiah 7:14 NIV

Fulfillment

This is how the birth of Jesus Christ came about: His mother Mary was pledged to be married to Joseph, but before they came together, she was found to be with child through the Holy Spirit.

Matthew 1:18 NIV
(Also Luke 1:26-35)

MASSACRE OF BABIES

Prophecy

Thus says the LORD: "A voice is heard in Ramah, lamentation and bitter weeping. Rachel is weeping for her children; she refuses to be comforted for her children, because they are not."

Jeremiah 31:15 RSV

Fulfillment

Herod, when he saw that he had been tricked by the wise men, was in a furious rage, and he sent and killed all the male children in Bethlehem and in all that region who were two years old or under, according to the time which he had ascertained from the wise men.

Matthew 2:16 RSV
(Also Matthew 2:17,18)

FLIGHT TO EGYPT

Prophecy

When Israel was a child, I loved him, and out of Egypt I called my son.

Hosea 11:1 RSV

Fulfillment

Then Joseph got up, took the child and his mother by night, and went to Egypt, and remained there until the death of Herod. This was to fulfill what had been spoken by the Lord through the prophet, "Out of Egypt I have called my son."

Matthew 2:14,15 NRSV

FORERUNNER OF THE MESSIAH

Prophecy

"Behold, I am going to send my messenger, and he will clear the way before me. And the Lord, whom you seek, will suddenly come to his temple; and the messenger of the covenant, in whom you delight, behold, he is coming," says the LORD of hosts.

Malachi 3:1 NASB
(Also Isaiah 40:3)

Fulfillment

"This is the one about whom it is written,
'Behold, I send my messenger ahead of you,
Who will prepare your way before you.'"

Luke 7:27 NASB
(Also Luke 1:17; John 1:23)

MINISTRY IN GALILEE

Prophecy

There will be no gloom for those who were in anguish. In the former time he brought into contempt the land of Zebulun and the land of Naphtali, but in the latter time he will make glorious the way of the sea, the land beyond the Jordan, Galilee of the nations.

The people who walked in darkness have seen a great light; those who lived in a land of deep darkness—on them light has shined.

Isaiah 9:1,2 NRSV

Fulfillment

He left Nazareth and made his home in Capernaum by the sea, in the territory of Zebulun and Naphtali, so that what had been spoken through the prophet Isaiah might be fulfilled.

Matthew 4:13,14 NRSV

AS A PROPHET

Prophecy

"The LORD your God will raise up for you a prophet like me from among you, from your countrymen, you shall listen to him."

Deuteronomy 18:15 NASB

Fulfillment

Therefore when the people saw the sign which he had performed, they said, "This is truly the Prophet who is to come into the world."

John 6:14 NASB
(Also Acts 3:19-26)

PRIEST IN THE ORDER OF MELCHIZEDEK

Prophecy

The LORD has sworn and will not change his mind: "You are a priest forever, in the order of Melchizedek."

Psalm 110:4 NIV

Fulfillment

Jesus, who went before us, has entered on our behalf. He has become a high priest forever, in the order of Melchizedek.

Hebrews 6:20 NIV
(Also Hebrews 5:5,6; 7:15-17)

SOME OF HIS CHARACTERISTICS

Prophecy
> The Spirit of the LORD shall rest upon him,
> The Spirit of wisdom and understanding,
> The Spirit of counsel and might,
> The Spirit of knowledge and of the fear of the
> LORD.
>
> *Isaiah 11:2 NKJV*
> *(Also Isaiah 61:1)*

Fulfillment
> And Jesus increased in wisdom and stature, and in
> favor with God and men.
>
> *Luke 2:52 NKJV*
> *(Also Luke 4:18)*

REJECTED BY HIS OWN PEOPLE

Prophecy
> He is despised and rejected of men; a man of sorrows, and acquainted with grief: and we hid as it were our faces from him; he was despised, and we esteemed him not.
>
> *Isaiah 53:3 KJV*

Fulfillment
> He came to his own, and his own did not receive
> him.
>
> *John 1:11 NKJV*
> *(Also John 5:43; Luke 17:25; 23:18)*

TRIUMPHANT ENTRY

Prophecy

Rejoice greatly, O daughter of Zion! Shout aloud, O daughter of Jerusalem! Lo, your king comes to you; triumphant and victorious is he, humble and riding on an ass, on a colt the foal of an ass.

Zechariah 9:9 RSV

Fulfillment

So they took branches of palm trees and went out to meet him, crying, "Hosanna! Blessed is he who comes in the name of the Lord, even the King of Israel!" And Jesus found a young ass and sat upon it.

John 12:13,14 RSV
(Also Matthew 21:1-11)

BETRAYED BY A FRIEND

Prophecy

Even my bosom friend in whom I trusted, who ate of my bread, has lifted his heel against me.

Psalm 41:9 RSV

Fulfillment

Then Judas Iscariot, who was one of the twelve, went to the chief priests in order to betray him to them.

Mark 14:10 RSV
(Also Luke 22:47,48)

SOLD FOR THIRTY PIECES OF SILVER

Prophecy

I told them, "If you think it best, give me my pay;
but if not, keep it." So they paid me thirty pieces
of silver.

Zechariah 11:12 NIV

Fulfillment

Then one of the Twelve—the one called Judas
Iscariot—went to the chief priests and asked,
"What are you willing to give me if I hand him
over to you?" So they counted out for him thirty
silver coins.

Matthew 26:14,15 NIV

POTTER'S FIELD BOUGHT WITH THE MONEY

Prophecy

The LORD said to me, "Throw it to the potter"—
the handsome price at which they priced me! So I
took the thirty pieces of silver and threw them into
the house of the LORD to the potter.

Zechariah 11:13 NIV

Fulfillment

Judas threw the money into the temple and left.
Then he went away and hanged himself. The chief
priests picked up the coins and said, "It is against

the law to put this into the treasury, since it is
blood money." So they decided to use the money
to buy the potter's field as a burial place for foreigners.

Matthew 27:5-7 NIV

THE BETRAYER'S OFFICE TO BE
TAKEN BY ANOTHER

Prophecy

When he is judged, let him be found guilty, and
let his prayer become sin. Let his days be few, and
let another take his office.

Psalm 109:7,8 NKJV

Fulfillment

And they prayed and said, "You, O Lord, who
know the hearts of all, show which of these two
you have chosen to take part in this ministry and
apostleship from which Judas by transgression fell,
that he might go to his own place." And they cast
their lots, and the lot fell on Matthias. And he was
numbered with the eleven apostles.

Acts 1:24-26 NKJV

ACCUSED BY FALSE WITNESSES

Prophecy

Do not deliver me over to the desire of my adver-
saries,
For false witnesses have risen against me,

And such as breathe out violence.

Psalm 27:12 NASB
(Also Psalm 35:11)

Fulfillment

The chief priests and the whole Council kept trying to obtain false testimony against Jesus, so that they might put him to death. They did not find any, even though many false witnesses came forward. But later on two came forward, and said, "This man stated, 'I am able to destroy the temple of God and to rebuild it in three days.'"

Matthew 26:59-61 NASB

SILENT WHEN ACCUSED

Prophecy

He was oppressed and he was afflicted,
Yet he did not open his mouth;
Like a lamb that is led to slaughter,
And like a sheep that is silent before its shearers,
So he did not open his mouth.

Isaiah 53:7 NASB
(Also Psalm 38:13,14)

Fulfillment

The high priest stood up and said to him, "Do you not answer? What is it that these men are testifying against you?" But Jesus kept silent.

Matthew 26:62,63 NASB

HATED WITHOUT A CAUSE

Prophecy

Those who hate me without a cause are more than
the hairs of my head;
Those who would destroy me are powerful, being
wrongfully my enemies;
What I did not steal, I then have to restore.

Psalm 69:4 NASB
(Also Psalm 109:3-5)

Fulfillment

"He who hates me hates my Father also. If I had
not done among them the works which no one
else did, they would have no sin; but now they
have seen and also hated both me and my Father.
But this happened that the word might be fulfilled
which is written in their law, 'They hated me without a cause.'"

John 15:23-25 NKJV

SUFFERED VICARIOUSLY

Prophecy

Surely he has borne our infirmities and carried our
diseases; yet we accounted him stricken, struck
down by God, and afflicted. But he was wounded
for our transgressions, crushed for our iniquities; upon him was the punishment that made us
whole, and by his bruises we are healed.

Isaiah 53:4,5 NRSV
(Also Isaiah 53:6,12)

Fulfillment

They brought to him many who were possessed with demons; and he cast out the spirits with a word, and cured all who were sick. This was to fulfill what had been spoken through the prophet Isaiah, "He took our infirmities and bore our diseases."

Matthew 8:16,17 NRSV
(Also Romans 4:25; 1 Corinthians 15:3)

CRUCIFIED WITH SINNERS

Prophecy

I will divide him a portion with the great, and he shall divide the spoil with the strong, because he poured out his soul unto death, and he was numbered with the transgressors, and he bore the sin of many, and made intercession for the transgressors.

Isaiah 53:12 NKJV

Fulfillment

Two robbers were crucified with him, one on the right and another on the left.

Matthew 27:38 NKJV

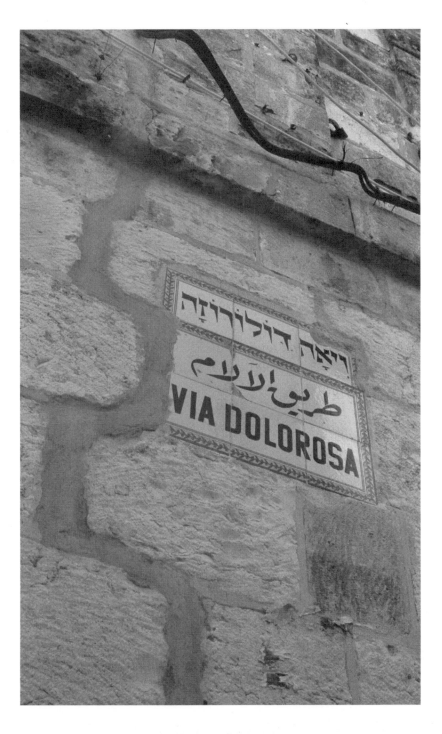

HANDS AND FEET PIERCED

Prophecy

Dogs have surrounded me; a band of evil men has encircled me, they have pierced my hands and my feet.

Psalm 22:16 NIV
(Also Zechariah 12:10)

Fulfillment

He said to Thomas, "Put your finger here; see my hands. Reach out your hand and put it into my side. Stop doubting and believe."

John 20:27 NIV
(Also John 19:37; 20:25,26)

MOCKED AND INSULTED

Prophecy

I am a worm and not a man, scorned by men and despised by the people. All who see me mock me; they hurl insults, shaking their heads: "He trusts in the LORD; let the LORD rescue him. Let him deliver him, since he delights in him."

Psalm 22:6-8 NIV

Fulfillment

Those who passed by hurled insults at him, shaking their heads and saying, "You who are going to destroy the temple and build it in three days, save yourself! Come down from the cross, if you are the

Son of God!"

Matthew 27:39,40 NIV
(Also Matthew 27:41-44; Mark 15:29-32)

GIVEN GALL AND VINEGAR

Prophecy

They put gall in my food and gave me vinegar for my thirst.

Psalm 69:21 NIV

Fulfillment

A jar of wine vinegar was there, so they soaked a sponge in it, put the sponge on a stalk of the hyssop plant, and lifted it to Jesus' lips.

John 19:29 NIV
(Also Matthew 27:34,48)

HEARS PROPHETIC WORDS REPEATED IN MOCKERY

Prophecy

"He committed his cause to the LORD; let him deliver him, let him rescue him, for he delights in him!"

Psalm 22:8 RSV

Fulfillment

"He trusts in God; let God deliver him now, if he desires him; for he said, 'I am the Son of God.'"

Matthew 27:43 RSV

PRAYS FOR HIS ENEMIES

Prophecy

In return for my love they accuse me, even while I make prayer for them.

Psalm 109:4 NRSV
(Also Isaiah 53:12)

Fulfillment

Jesus said, "Father, forgive them; for they do not know what they are doing." And they cast lots to divide his clothing.

Luke 23:34 NRSV

HIS SIDE WAS PIERCED

Prophecy

"I will pour out on the house of David and on the inhabitants of Jerusalem, the Spirit of grace and of supplication, so that they will look on me whom they have pierced; and they will mourn for him, as one mourns for an only son, and they will weep bitterly over him like the bitter weeping over a firstborn."

Zechariah 12:10 NASB

Fulfillment

One of the soldiers pierced his side with a spear, and immediately blood and water came out.

John 19:34 NASB

SOLDIERS CAST LOTS FOR HIS GARMENTS

Prophecy

They divide my garments among them,
And for my clothing they cast lots.

Psalm 22:18 NASB

Fulfillment

And they crucified him, and divided up his garments among themselves, casting lots for them to decide what each man should take.

Mark 15:24 NASB
(Also John 19:24)

BURIED WITH THE RICH

Prophecy

He was assigned a grave with the wicked, and with the rich in his death, though he had done no violence, nor was any deceit in his mouth.

Isaiah 53:9 NIV

Fulfillment

As evening approached, there came a rich man from Arimathea, named Joseph, who had himself become a disciple of Jesus. Going to Pilate, he asked for Jesus' body, and Pilate ordered that it be given to him. Joseph took the body, wrapped it in a clean linen cloth, and placed it in his own new tomb that he had cut out of the rock. He rolled a

big stone in front of the entrance to the tomb and went away.

Matthew 27:57-60 NIV

HIS RESURRECTION

Prophecy

For you will not abandon my soul to Sheol;
Nor will you allow Your Holy One to undergo decay.

Psalm 16:10 NASB

Fulfillment

Behold, Jesus met them and greeted them. And they came up and took hold of his feet and worshiped him.

Matthew 28:9 NASB
(Also Luke 24:36-48; Matthew 16:21)

HIS ASCENSION

Prophecy

When you ascended on high, you led captives in your train; you received gifts from men, even from the rebellious—that you, O LORD God, might dwell there.

Psalm 68:18 NIV

Fulfillment

When he had led them out to the vicinity of Bethany, he lifted up his hands and blessed them.

While he was blessing them, he left them and was taken up into heaven.

Luke 24:50,51 NIV

Fulfillment

After the Lord Jesus had spoken to them, he was taken up into heaven and he sat at the right hand of God.

Mark 16:19 NIV
(Also Acts 1:9)

GETTING TO KNOW
THE MESSIAH

GETTING
TO KNOW
THE MESSIAH

The Scriptures say:

> "Surely I know the plans I have for you," says the
> LORD, "plans for your welfare and not for harm, to
> give you a future with hope. Then when you call
> upon me and come and pray to me, I will hear
> you. When you search for me, you will find me; if
> you seek me with all your heart."
>
> *Jeremiah 29:11-13 NRSV*

If your desire is to seek God, you can pray this simple
prayer:

> *Dear God, I know I have sinned. Please forgive*
> *me. I believe that Yeshua took my punishment. He*
> *died for me, but you raised him from the dead.*
> *Thank you for forgiving me and making me right-*
> *eous. Now I want to obey you, because you love me*
> *and you know what is best for me.*

Blessed is he whose transgressions are forgiven, whose sins are covered. Blessed is the man whose sin the LORD does not count against him and in whose spirit is no deceit.

Psalm 32:1,2 NIV

With joy you will draw water from the wells of salvation. In that day you will say: "Give thanks to the LORD, call on his name; make known among the nations what he has done, and proclaim that his name is exalted. Sing to the LORD, for he has done glorious things; let this be known to all the world. Shout aloud and sing for joy, people of Zion, for great is the Holy One of Israel among you."

Isaiah 12:3-6 NIV

THE STORY BEHIND
THE PROPHETS SPEAK

The Prophets Speak was first published in Russian as a special feature in our Bible for Russian Jews, with its striking cover illustrations of the Star of David and a menorah.

The "Star of David Bible", as it is affectionately called, began as a simple idea in 1993:

> *If only the Russian Jews could see for themselves how much God loves them and what wonderful plans he has for them. If only they could read God's Word for themselves...*

That thought quickly led to another: They need Bibles, but a Bible with a difference—a Bible to touch their hearts.

Today, the outcome is known to Russian Jewish people the world over. More than a quarter of a million of this complete Bible have been distributed, and Russian Jews who might never have picked up a traditional Bible are reading God's Word for themselves.

The selection of Scriptures in The Prophets Speak is included in the Russian "Jewish" Bible before Genesis and after Revelation.

The Prophets Speak is also published in Chinese and Finnish.

FOR MORE INFORMATION,
PLEASE VISIT OUR WEBSITE AT
WWW.MEDIASERVE.ORG